DOMINOES

Rip Van Winkle
and The Legend
of Sleepy Hollow

STARTER LEVEL   250 HEADWORDS

OXFORD
UNIVERSITY PRESS

Great Clarendon Street, Oxford OX2 6DP

Oxford University Press is a department of the University of Oxford.
It furthers the University's objective of excellence in research, scholarship,
and education by publishing worldwide in

Oxford New York

Auckland Cape Town Dar es Salaam Hong Kong Karachi
Kuala Lumpur Madrid Melbourne Mexico City Nairobi
New Delhi Shanghai Taipei Toronto

With offices in

Argentina Austria Brazil Chile Czech Republic France Greece
Guatemala Hungary Italy Japan Poland Portugal Singapore
South Korea Switzerland Thailand Turkey Ukraine Vietnam

OXFORD and OXFORD ENGLISH are registered trade marks of
Oxford University Press in the UK and in certain other countries

This edition © Oxford University Press 2010

The moral rights of the author have been asserted

Database right Oxford University Press (maker)

First published in Dominoes 2002

2014 2013 2012 2011

10 9 8 7

ISBN: 978 0 19 424702 3 BOOK
ISBN: 978 0 19 424666 8 BOOK AND MULTIROM PACK
MULTIROM NOT AVAILABLE SEPARATELY

Printed in China

This book is printed on paper from certified and well-managed sources.

ACKNOWLEDGEMENTS

Illustrations by: Ashley Smith (cover), Thomas Sperling (interior).

The publisher would like to thank the following for permission to reproduce photographs: Bridgeman
Art Library Ltd pp iv (Pocahontas engraving by Simon de Passe (1595–1647)/Private
Collection), 26 (A Peaceful Summer Day by Konstantin Rodko (1908–95) / Private Collection,
New York, USA); Corbis pp iv (George Washington/Francis G. Mayer), iv (President Abraham
Lincoln), iv (Henry Hudson/Bettmann), 13 (Henry Hudson/Bettmann); Getty Images p 44
(Alien/Antonio Rosario/Image Bank); Kobal Collection p 42 (A Christmas Carol/MGM);
National Portrait Gallery Picture Library p iv (George III); NHPA p 44 (Bat/Stephen Dalton);
OUP pp iv (map of USA/Geoatlas), 43 (Man in crowd/Digital Vision); Oxford Scientific (OSF)
pp 42 (Feral cat/London Scientific Films), 43 (Tarantula/David Fox), 44 (Earthworm), 44 (Rat/
Liz Bomford), 44 (Human skull/R.L.Manuel), 44 (Centipede/David M Dennis), 44 (Assassin
bug/David M Dennis); Robert Harding World Imagery p 42 (Snake); Science Photo Library
p42 (Fear of flying/Oscar Burriel); The Art Archive p 12 (Flying Fish/Musée de la Marine
Paris/Gianni Dagli Orti).

DOMINOES

Series Editors: Bill Bowler and Sue Parminter

Rip Van Winkle and The Legend of Sleepy Hollow

Washington Irving

Text adaptation by Alan Hines

Illustrated by Thomas Sperling

Washington Irving (1783–1859) was one of the first American writers. He was born in New York City and studied law there. From 1815 until 1832 he lived in Europe, and while he was there he published most of his successful stories, including *The Legend of Sleepy Hollow* and *Rip Van Winkle* (1819). On his return to the USA he travelled west into Indian territory, a journey he described in *A Tour of the Prairies* (1835).

OXFORD
UNIVERSITY PRESS

BEFORE READING

1 This story comes from North America.

Match the names with the pictures and the descriptions.

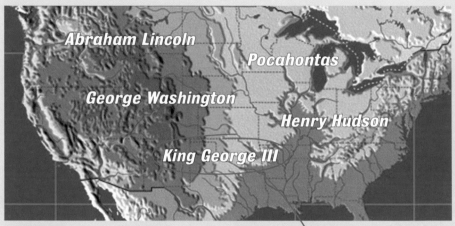

Abraham Lincoln

Pocahontas

George Washington

Henry Hudson

King George III

a The first President of the USA. (1732–1799)

b The sixteenth President of the USA. (1809–1865)

c An American Indian princess. (1595–1617)

d The last British king of North America. (1738–1820)

e The first white man – working for Holland – to visit different places in North America. (1570–1611)

2 Three of these people are in the story of Rip Van Winkle. Which three?

RIP VAN WINKLE

Chapter 1 The Catskill **Mountains** change colour at different times of the year. Many people think that they are **magic** mountains.

It is 1769. In a village near the Catskills lives a friendly man. His name is Rip Van Winkle. The village children love him.

---

mountains very big hills

magic not usual, and with something that you can't understand

Rip loves doing nothing all day.

But when the men of the village ask Rip for help on their **farms**, he always goes and helps them.

And when the women of the village ask Rip for help, he never says no.

Rip is always ready to do his **neighbours'** work – but he never works on *his* farm!

farm a house with land in the country

neighbour a person who lives near you

The Van Winkles have two **wild** children – Rip and Judith. Young Rip always wears his father's old **clothes**.

Morning and night Mrs Van Winkle tells him that he is **lazy**.

Rip never answers her. This makes her angrier.

One day, Rip leaves his **wife** at the farm. He calls his dog, Wolf, and they go for a walk in the mountains.

wild not quiet and not good; not staying where you want

lazy not wanting to work

wife a woman living with a man

clothes people wear these

3

In the late afternoon, Rip sits on one of the mountains. For a long time, he watches the beautiful Hudson **River**.

Soon the sky is dark. Rip's wife always gets angry when he comes home late, so he must leave now.

When he goes down the mountain, Rip meets a **stranger**. The man has something on his back.

The stranger isn't very tall. He's fat, his hair is wild, and he's wearing old Dutch clothes. He wants Rip to carry the **barrel**.

river water that moves through the country in a long line

stranger someone that you don't know

barrel a tall round box; you put things to drink in it

Rip walks up the mountain with the man. Sometimes he carries the barrel to help him. The stranger says nothing.

After a time, they meet a number of men in the mountains. They are all playing an old Dutch **game**, and wearing old Dutch clothes.

The man with the barrel gives them all a drink. Everything is quiet. Nobody smiles, and nobody speaks.

When the men begin to play again, Rip has a drink. He feels thirsty, so he drinks more and more.

Soon Rip is tired. His eyes close, and he goes to sleep.

game something that you play; tennis and football are games

READING CHECK

Choose the correct pictures.

a Rip van Winkle
lives with his . . .

 ✔

b He lives in a . . .

c One autumn day he goes
with his dog Wolf to . . .

d Some . . . there give him
a drink and he goes to sleep.

WORD WORK

**1 Find nine more words
from Chapter 1 in
the barrel.**

```
B M A G I C M S
F F I W J Q L O T Y
N E I G H B O U R S
N R I V E R T N A A
N B A I I Z H T N F
U W I L D X E A G A
U L G A M E S I E R
V C G Z L Q T N R M
J K Y S W Z S B
```

2 Use words from Activity 1 to complete the sentences.

a

I love working a lot.

No, you don't. You're really .....lazy.....

b

Do you know him?

No, I don't. He's a .... here.

Do you like the people in the house next to your house?

c

Yes, I do. They're very good ....

d

I don't like tennis.

Oh! Do you like any ....?

e

Where is he?

Fishing in the ...., I think.

What *are* you wearing?

f

Some new .... Do you like them?

Would you like to live in a little house in the town?

g

No. I like living on a .... in the country.

Those little hills are nice.

h

They aren't little hills. They're big ....!

GUESS WHAT

The next chapter is twenty years later.
What happens?
Put these things in order.
Number them 1–6.

☐ Rip feels old.

☐ Rip wakes up.

☐ Rip talks to his daughter.

☐ Rip hears his wife is dead.

☐ Rip sees his son.

☐ Rip sees different things in the village.

Chapter 2 When Rip opens his eyes, it's a sunny morning. 'Oh, no!' he cries. 'My wife doesn't like me to sleep away from home!'

Rip remembers his night on the mountain. He stands up, but finds he can't move very easily. And where's Wolf?

In the village, some children laugh at him. The buildings, the people, and their clothes are all different. Rip feels afraid.

He finds his house – with no windows or door! And where are his wife and children? Rip doesn't understand.

Just then, he puts his hand to his face, and finds he has a long white **beard**!

beard the hair on a man's face

8

He runs to the village **inn**. Over the door, the picture of **King** George has new clothes and a new name: GEORGE WASHINGTON.

Rip doesn't know any of the people in front of the inn. 'Does nobody here know Rip Van Winkle?' he asks.

'Yes. That's Rip Van Winkle, next to the tree,' one man says. Rip sees a young man in *his* clothes. 'Is that me?' he thinks.

But before Old Rip can speak to him, a young woman next to him says to her **baby**, 'Quiet, Rip!' He hears the baby's name and turns to her.

inn an old name for a hotel where people can eat, drink and stay

king the most important man in a country; the king here is George III, King of England from 1760

baby a very young child

'What's your name?' he asks. 'Judith,' she answers. 'And your father's name?' 'Rip Van Winkle,' she says.

'And where is he?' 'Nobody knows,' she says, 'After his walk into the mountains twenty years **ago**.' 'And your mother?' Rip asks. 'She's dead,' Judith says.

Then Rip laughs. 'I'm your father!' he cries. 'Young Rip Van Winkle then. Old Rip Van Winkle now. Don't any of you know me?'

An old woman looks into Rip's face. 'Yes, it is Rip Van Winkle!' she says. 'After twenty years. **Welcome** home, old friend!'

ago before now

welcome we say this when someone arrives and we are happy to see them

Rip tells his story of the men in Dutch clothes, and their **strange** game in the mountains. Some people think he's **mad**.

But one old man cries 'I think Old Rip's story is true! Every twenty years, they say, the **ghost** of the Dutch **explorer**, Henry Hudson, comes back with his men to the Catskills. Those strangers in old Dutch clothes were Hudson and his men!'

So Old Rip goes to live with Judith. And his son goes to work on the old farm sometimes!

And every day, without his wife there to tell him he's lazy, Old Rip goes to the inn, has a drink, and tells his strange story to the visitors staying there.

strange not usual

mad thinking things that are not true

ghost a dead person that a living person sees or hears

explorer someone who visits countries before other people

READING CHECK

Match the two parts of these sentences.

a It's a sunny morning . . .
b Rip can't find . . .
c The village, the people there,
and their clothes . . .
d Rip's house . . .
e The old picture over the inn
door of George III . . .
f Rip's son is now . . .
g Rip's daughter is now . . .
h Rip's wife . . .
i Old Rip goes to live . . .
j He goes to the *George Washington*
for a drink every day . . .

1 look different to Rip's eyes.
2 with Judith.
3 when Rip opens his eyes
on the mountain.
4 is now a picture of George
Washington.
5 his dog Wolf.
6 is dead.
7 a man.
8 has nobody in it.
9 and tells his story to
everybody there.
10 a woman with a young son.

WORD WORK

1 Find nine more words from Chapter 2 in the wordsquare.

Use the words from Activity 1 to complete the sentences.

a Henry Hudson's the name of a famous ..explorer.. .

b I like reading about .... George III of England.

c Their youngest child is only a little ....

d My grandfather has got a long white ....

e Let's have lunch at that nice old .... in the village.

f We usually go to bed early, so it feels .... to stay up late.

g My grandfather thinks he's George Washington.
He's really ....

h The book is about America 180 years ....

i 'This is my first time in New York.'
'Is it? .... to New York, then!'

j I'm sure there's a .... in this house. You can hear
someone walking about at night when nobody's there.

GUESS WHAT

What happens after the end of the story? Tick three boxes.

a ☐ RIP WRITES A BOOK ABOUT HIS STRANGE 20 YEAR SLEEP

b ☐ A MAN FROM NEW YORK — DIEDRICH KNICKERBOCKER —
WRITES A BOOK ABOUT RIP'S STRANGE 20 YEAR SLEEP

c ☐ WASHINGTON IRVING FINDS DIEDRICH'S PAPERS WHEN
HE DIES. HE PUTS RIP'S STORY IN HIS NEXT BOOK

d ☐ WASHINGTON IRVING HEARS RIP'S STORY FROM RIP'S
GRANDSON AND PUTS IT INTO ONE OF HIS BOOKS

e ☐ RIP VAN WINKLE BECOMES FAMOUS

BEFORE READING

1 What are the good things about living in the country? What are the bad things? Tick the boxes.

		😊 good	😞 bad
a	Everybody knows their neighbours.	☐	☐
b	There's nobody new.	☐	☐
c	It's very quiet.	☐	☐
d	Nothing exciting happens.	☐	☐
e	People know everything about you.	☐	☐

2 This story is about a number of people living in the country. Look at the people and complete the sentences. Use these words: *loves, hates, likes, is afraid of.*

Ichabod: the teacher	Katrina: the rich farmer's daughter	A ghost with no head	Van Tassel: the rich farmer	Brom: Katrina's friend

a Ichabod .... Katrina.

b Katrina .... Ichabod.

c Katrina .... Brom.

d Brom .... Ichabod.

e Ichabod .... Brom.

f Ichabod .... the ghost with no head.

g Van Tassel .... Ichabod.

h Van Tassel .... Brom.

i Van Tassel .... Katrina.

j Brom .... Katrina.

3 Which people are happy at the end of the story? Which people are unhappy? Why?

The Legend of SLEEPY HOLLOW

Chapter 1 Let's go back into the past – far back, to the good old days of America. Tarry Town is a little village on the Hudson River.

Not far away, there's a quiet **valley**. Sleepy Hollow is its name.

People there tell many stories about magic and ghosts. The most important of these is the **legend** of a **Headless Horseman**.

legend an old story – half true, half not true

valley land between two hills

headless without a head

horseman a man on a horse

Ichabod Crane teaches the children in Sleepy Hollow. He's tall and **thin**, and he's got long arms, big hands and feet, a little head, and cold green eyes.

The students in his **school** usually work well. When they don't, he hits them with a big **stick**.

After school, he walks some of the younger schoolboys home. He likes seeing their beautiful older sisters and meeting their mothers (and getting nice things to eat)!

Ichabod eats, sleeps, and lives with the families of his students. After a week in one house, he puts all his things into a little bag and moves to the next family.

Ichabod /ˈɪkəbɑːd/

thin not fat

school students learn here

stick a long thin piece of wood

From time to time, he helps the men with their work on the farm. He always looks for easy things to do, here and there.

At other times, he stays with the young children in the house – telling them stories or getting them to sleep. This makes their mothers very happy.

In the evenings, Ichabod teaches singing to make some **extra** money. On Sundays, he **directs** his singers in the **church**. He feels very important then.

Country women usually think teachers are interesting. Teachers know more than farmers, they speak better, and they like nice things, too.

extra more than usual

direct to make people begin and stop singing

church Christian people go here to pray

Ichabod can talk to young women very easily. The farmers' sons watch and listen, but they are afraid to speak in front of him.

After school, Ichabod reads for hours about **witches** and **black magic**. Before he knows it, it's night time and he can't see his book!

When he walks home, all the little noises in the night make him feel afraid. Then he begins to sing, and this makes him feel **brave** again.

 **witch** a woman who can fly through the sky and do bad things

 **black magic** bad magic

brave not afraid

Ichabod likes to listen to the old women of the village when they tell stories of ghosts and **haunted** houses. He loves the legend of the Headless Horseman.

Ghost stories are exciting when he's sitting in a nice, warm room. But they're frightening when he's walking home later on a cold, dark night.

He often thinks that he hears the Headless Horseman not far behind him!

haunted where people see lots of ghosts

READING CHECK

Correct six more mistakes.

The story begins in Tarry Town, a village on the ~~Mississippi~~ *Hudson* River. The mountain of Sleepy Hollow is near Tarry Town. Nobody likes ghost stories in Sleepy Hollow. Ichabod Crane works in the inn there. He has a house in the valley. He likes nice food, and listening to young women when they tell ghost stories. He doesn't like doing farm work very much. He really likes reading love stories.

WORD WORK

1 These words don't match the pictures. Correct them.

a a ~~horseman~~ *valley*

b a stick

c a valley

d a church

e a school

f a witch

2 Find the words in Ichabod's stick to complete the sentences.

THINLEGENDSDIRECTEXTRABRAVEHAUNTEDHEADLESS

a   Ichabod does ...extra.... work in the evenings for more money.

b   He isn't fat, he's ....

c   Brom isn't afraid of ghosts. He's very ....

d   Sleepy Hollow is a .... place. It has lots of ghosts.

e   I think the story of Hercules is the best of all the old Greek ....

f   That ghost is .... It's got its head under its arm.

g   I'd like to .... people singing in church.

GUESS WHAT

What happens in the next chapter? Tick the boxes.

a   Ichabod meets . . .
  ☐ a ghost.
  ☐ a beautiful young woman.
  ☐ a handsome young man.

b   Ichabod . . .
  ☐ fights with the young man.
  ☐ runs away from the ghost.
  ☐ tries to be the young
      woman's good friend.

Chapter 2 In the day, Ichabod forgets about ghosts and witches. The only thing he thinks about is Katrina Van Tassel. He's **under** her **spell**.

The Van Tassels have the biggest farm in the valley. When Ichabod walks past, he always stops to look at its **fields** and its farmhouse. Who gets all this when her father Baltus dies? Katrina, of course.

Katrina is Baltus Van Tassel's beautiful young daughter. She's eighteen and an **only child**.

Ichabod thinks a lot about the farmer's beautiful daughter. He knows he must make Katrina love him!

---

under somebody's spell only thinking of one person

field a piece of land that a farm has

only child a person with no brothe or sisters

A number of the farmers' sons like Katrina, too.

The most important of these young men is Brom Van Brunt. He's big and **strong**, and he's always ready for a **fight** or a laugh.

When the other farmers' sons see Brom's horse in front of Van Tassel's farm in the evening, they know that Brom is visiting Katrina.

But Ichabod doesn't **lose hope**. He begins visiting Van Tassel's farm every day to help Katrina with her singing.

strong with a body that works well   **fight** when someone hits people again and again   **lose hope** to stop thinking that something nice can happen

In the late afternoon, Baltus smokes happily and Katrina and Ichabod walk under the trees. Brom watches angrily. But nobody sees him.

Brom and his friends begin to **play tricks on** Ichabod.

When Ichabod teaches Katrina to sing, Brom teaches his dog to **howl**.

At night, they move all the books and chairs in the school. In the morning, Ichabod arrives. He begins to think all the witches in the country meet in his school after **nightfall**.

play tricks on somebody to do bad things and laugh at somebody **howl** to cry (of a dog) **nightfall** the time when night begin

One afternoon Baltus Van Tassel's **servant** arrives at the school door. He asks Ichabod to go to a **party** that evening at Van Tassel's farm.

Ichabod can't wait! 'You can leave school an hour early today,' he tells all the schoolboys.

He runs back to his room and puts on his best black **suit**.

He **borrows** a tired old horse for the night. The horse's name is Gunpowder and he usually works in the fields.

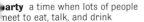

servant a person who works for someone rich

party a time when lots of people meet to eat, talk, and drink

suit a jacket and trousers of one colour

borrow to take for a short time

READING CHECK

Choose the correct words to complete the sentences.

a Ichabod thinks of Katrina van Tassel / The Headless Horseman in the day.

b Katrina's father Baltus Van Tassel is / isn't very rich.

c Brom Van Brunt visits Ichabod / Katrina at home.

d Ichabod teaches Katrina to speak French / sing.

e Brom is angry and does bad things to Katrina / Ichabod.

f Baltus Van Tassel / Brom asks Ichabod to come to his house.

g Ichabod is afraid / happy to go there.

WORD WORK

1 Correct the mistakes.
All the correct words are in Chapter 2.

a Ichabod is under Katrina's ~~smell~~. *spell*

b It's not nice to play bricks on your friends.

c Can I barrow your pen for a minute?

d Van Tassel's farm has got lots of big shields.

e Don't lose rope. I think the story finishes happily.

f Brom's a very string man – with big arms and legs.

Find the words in Baltus Van Tassel's pipe
to match the underlined words in the sentences.

I like your new green <u>jacket and trousers</u>. ......*suit*......

They like <u>hitting people</u> a lot! ....

<u>Boys or girls with no brothers or sisters</u> often spend a lot of time
with their mothers and fathers. ....

We're having a <u>time to eat, drink and dance to music</u> at my house
this Saturday. ....

We must leave at <u>the time when night begins</u>. ....

Can you hear that dog <u>crying</u> in the garden. ....

He's a <u>man working in a rich person's house</u>. ....

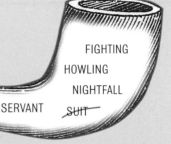

FIGHTING

HOWLING

NIGHTFALL

ONLY CHILDREN

PARTY

SERVANT

~~SUIT~~

GUESS WHAT

What happens at the party? Tick three boxes.

a ☐ Ichabod spends time with Katrina.

b ☐ 'Fight me!' says Brom to Ichabod.

c ☐ Brom tells a ghost story.

d ☐ 'I love you,' says Ichabod to Katrina.

e ☐ 'I love you,' says Katrina to Ichabod.

Chapter 3 It is early evening when Ichabod arrives at Van Tassel's farmhouse. All the farmers from the **neighbourhood** are at the party with their families.

When Brom arrives, everyone is happy to see him. (Not Ichabod, of course!) Brom's horse is big and strong. His name is Daredevil, and only Brom can **ride** him.

Ichabod feels happy when he sees all the good things to eat and drink in the farmhouse. Then he sees Katrina talking with Brom and he feels angry again.

Someone begins playing **music** in the next room. Ichabod knows Katrina loves to **dance**. He smiles when he remembers Brom can't dance.

neighbourhood all the houses near your house

music people listen or dance to this

dance to move your body and feet to music

ride to go on a horse

Ichabod knows he sings well, and he also dances wonderfully!

When the dancing finishes, people begin to talk about the ghosts in Sleepy Hollow.

Brom tells the most exciting story. 'Some nights when I ride through the village, the Headless Horseman **follows** me,' he says.

'When I get to the **bridge** in front of the old church,' Brom goes on, 'The Headless Horseman always stops. His horse can't **step** on to the bridge! And the rider and horse **disappear** in a **flash** of **fire**.'

---

ollow to go after someone

ridge people can go across a
iver on this

step to put your foot down

disappear to go away suddenly

flash a sudden light

fire this is red and hot, and it burns

Soon the party is over, and everybody begins to leave. Before Ichabod goes, he tells Katrina about his love for her.

But something goes badly wrong, and soon Ichabod leaves Van Tassel's farmhouse quickly and quietly.

Without looking left or right, he rides away through Sleepy Hollow.

The night is very dark. Ichabod thinks about Katrina and he feels terrible. Then he hears a noise.

He looks back over his **shoulder** and sees something big, black and frightening in the dark night behind him.

He's very afraid. At first, he can't speak. In the end he asks **weakly**, 'Who are you?'

The **figure** doesn't answer.

shoulder this is between your arm and your neck

weakly not strongly

figure someone that you can't see very well

READING CHECK

Correct the mistakes.

after
a Brom arrives at Van Tassel's farm ~~before~~ Ichabod.

b Ichabod is very happy to see Brom there.

c Eating and drinking a lot makes Ichabod feel worse.

d Ichabod can't dance very well.

e Ichabod tells people about nights when the
Headless Horseman comes after him.

f Brom leaves Van Tassel's farm after Ichabod.

g When Ichabod leaves the farm, he feels angry.

h Something on a bicycle comes after him in the dark.

i He doesn't speak to it, but it speaks to him.

WORD WORK

**Use the words in the sandwiches
to complete the sentences.**

a I go horse ....riding.... every
weekend.

b Do you like listening to this
........................?

c Trains go over the road on a
....

d 'I'm cold.' 'Sit nearer the
........................, then.'

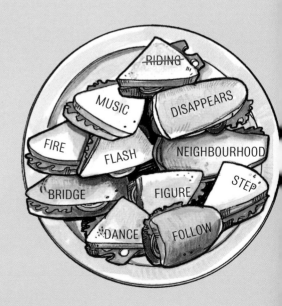

e 'Is there somebody at the end of the garden?' 'Yes. I can see a dark .... there, but who is it?'

f All the people living in the houses near us are our friends. We live in a very nice ....

g Our cat always .... out of the window when our dog comes into the room!

h 'How can we get up this mountain?' 'Shall I go first? Then you can .... me.'

i There was a sudden .... in the dark sky and it began to rain.

j 'Would you like to .... with me?' 'OK. But don't .... on my feet.'

GUESS WHAT

How does the story end? Use the names to complete the sentences.

Ichabod . . .   Brom . . .   The horseman . . .   Katrina . . .

a .... runs away.

b .... runs after Ichabod.

c .... feels afraid.

d .... suddenly can't sing very well.

e .... thinks the horseman can't get nearer.

f .... hits Ichabod with something.

g .... leaves Sleepy Hollow.

h .... stays in Sleepy Hollow.

Chapter 4 Then Ichabod **slaps** Gunpowder on the back and the old horse **gallops** away! The ghost follows them on his big black horse.

When Ichabod makes Gunpowder walk slowly, the ghost makes his horse walk slowly, too.

Usually, when Ichabod is afraid, he sings to feel braver. Now he opens his mouth but no noise comes out!

slap to hit with your open hand   **gallop** to move fast (on a horse)

When Ichabod gets to a hill, he looks back. Now he can see the ghost is headless! The rider's head is on the **saddle** in front of him.

At first, Ichabod is very afraid and can't move.

Then he slaps and **kicks** Gunpowder and makes him gallop away again! And the headless horseman follows him.

saddle the thing that you put on a horse's back to sit on

kick to hit with your feet

Soon Ichabod sees the church and the bridge through the trees. He remembers Brom's story. The ghost can't go across the bridge!

Ichabod gallops across the bridge and looks back over his shoulder.

The horseman takes his head in his hands and **throws** it at Ichabod! It **knocks** him down off his horse. Gunpowder and the headless horseman gallop away.

throw to make something move quickly from your hand through the air

knock to hit strongly

The next morning, people find Gunpowder near his home.

Nobody can find Ichabod. But they find his hat near the bridge. And they find a **pumpkin** in pieces near the hat.

Soon after Brom **marries** Katrina. When people tell the story of Ichabod Crane, Brom smiles. He laughs when they talk about the pumpkin near the bridge.

To this day, sitting in front of the fire, people in Sleepy Hollow like to tell ghost stories. And everyone's **favourite** is the legend of Ichabod Crane and the Headless Horseman.

pumpkin a big orange vegetable

marry to make someone your husband or wife

favourite the one that people like best

READING CHECK

Put the sentences in order. Number them 1–9.

a ☐ The horseman runs after Ichabod.

b ☐ Ichabod opens his mouth, but he can't sing.

c ☑ Ichabod runs away from the horseman.

d ☐ Ichabod rides over the bridge.

e ☐ A farmer finds Ichabod's horse the next day.

f ☐ Ichabod sees the figure has got no head.

g ☐ The headless horseman throws his head at Ichabod.

h ☐ People find Ichabod's hat near the bridge, but they can't find Ichabod.

i ☐ Brom can get nearer to Katrina without Ichabod in Sleepy Hollow.

WORD WORK

Use the words in the pumpkin to complete the sentences.

GALLOPING   KICK

KNOCK   FAVOURITE   MARRY

PUMPKIN   SADDLE   SLAP

THROW

a Do you want some ...pumpkin... soup?

Yes, please!
It's my ....

b OK. Now when I .... the ball to you,
you must .... it with your right foot!

c

What do I do when my horse is going really fast?

When you are ...., don't sit down in the .... Half stand up. That's very important.

e

Don't .... your sister off her horse!

I'm sorry, Mum. Please don't .... me!

d

Please .... me, Jill! I love you.

Oh, Sam. You must give me time to think about it.

GUESS WHAT

Which story do people in Sleepy Hollow like to tell about Ichabod?
Which is the true story?

a The headless horseman is really Brom with his coat over his head and a pumpkin in his hands, but Ichabod doesn't know that. Ichabod is so afraid he runs away from Sleepy Hollow and goes to live in New York.

b Ichabod runs away from the headless horseman, but the horseman runs faster and takes Ichabod away to his home under the valley. You can sometimes hear Ichabod's ghost moving about in the old school house.

PROJECT A

TWENTY YEARS
FROM NOW

1 **Rip Van Winkle sleeps for twenty years and then wakes up. Life can change a lot in twenty years. Match the pictures with the sentences.**

It's twenty years from now . . .

a ☐ Cars are smaller. People don't walk any more. They go by car all the time.

b ☐ People don't go to work. They work from home through the internet.

c ☐ People don't visit shops. They buy things through the internet.

d ☐ People don't read paper books. They read small computer books.

e ☐ People go on holiday to the moon.

f ☐ People have big 3D TVs at home.

g ☐ People have radios in their heads.

h ☐ People live longer. Most people live for 110 years.

Imagine that you sleep for twenty years.
Fill in the questionnaire.

SLEEPER QUESTIONNAIRE
What changes do you see?

In people's houses:

....
....
....
....

In people's lives:

....
....
....
....

In the way people work:

....
....
....
....

In what people do in their free time:

....
....
....
....

PROJECT B

What are you

1 **People are afraid of different things. Read and complete the poster using words from the box.**

dark	flying	ghosts
crowded places	snakes	spiders
thirteen	cats	

a I'm afraid of ....

b My aunt doesn't like ....

d My Dad doesn't like ....

c My grandmother is afraid of ....

42

afraid of?

13

g My Mum doesn't like the number ....

e My little sister is afraid of the ....

f My brother hates ....

h My best friend hates being in ....

2 Fill in the questionnaires on page 44.

3 What are you afraid of?

What about your family and friends?

**WHAT
ARE YOU
AFRAID OF?**

....

....

....

....

....

Name: ....

Relationship to you: ....

What is he/she afraid of? ....

....

....

Name: ....

Relationship to you: ....

What is he/she afraid of? ....

....

....

Name: ....

Relationship to you: ....

What is he/she afraid of? ....

....

....

Name: ....

Relationship to you: ....

What is he/she afraid of? ....

....

....

GRAMMAR CHECK

Adverbs of frequency

Adverbs of frequency tell us how often something happens.

He is always read to do his neighbours' work.

Adverbs of frequency usually come before the main verb, but after the verb be.

always	*Rip always goes and helps the villagers.*
usually	*Young Rip and Judith usually go to bed early.*
often	*Mrs Van Winkle often tells Rip that he is lazy.*
sometimes	*Rip sometimes carries the barrel for the stranger.*
never	*He never answers his wife.*

1 Choose the correct adverb of frequency and put it in the correct place in the sentences.

a The Catskill Mountains ∧change colour. (usually/sometimes) *sometimes*

b Rip helps the men of the village. (always/often)

c Rip's son wears his father's old clothes. (never/always)

d Rip answers his wife. (usually/never)

e Rip takes his dog for a walk in the mountains. (always/sometimes)

f Rip's wife gets angry when he comes home late. (always/never)

g After his night on the mountain, Old Rip sees his wife again. (often/never)

h Henry Hudson and his men come back to the Catskill Mountains. (sometimes/often)

i Young Rip works on the old farm. (usually/sometimes)

j Old Rip goes to the inn for a drink. (always/often)

GRAMMAR CHECK

Personal pronouns

We use the pronouns I, you, he, she, we, and they in place of people's names when they are the subject of a sentence.

Mrs Van Winkle is angry.	*She is angry.*
Rip has two children.	*He has two children.*
Young Rip and Judith are wild.	*They are wild.*
The dog is hungry.	*It is hungry.*

2 Complete the sentences with *I*, *you*, *he*, *she*, *we*, or *they*.

Mother: Young Rip! Judith! Rip! Where are a) ..you..?

Young Rip: Here b) .... am, mother!

Mother: Oh Rip! What are c) .... wearing?

Young Rip: This is father's old coat. d) .... doesn't wear it now.

Mother: Where's Judith, Rip?

Young Rip: e)............'s near the river with her friends. f) ....'re playing.

Mother: Find Judith, Rip, and bring her home quickly. g) ....'re all going to church soon. Now, where's your father?

Young Rip: Oh, h) .... know! i) ....'s under the apple tree!

Mother: What's j) .... doing there?

Young Rip: k) ....'s sleeping, of course! (Young Rip runs away.)

Mother: What a wild family! Well, l) ....'m going to church now. m) .... can come later. n) .... don't want to wait.

GRAMMAR CHECK

Sequencing words: at first, then, later, in the end, and at the same time

We use sequencing words like at first, then, later, and in the end to show the order of events in a story. Sequencing words usually come at the beginning of a sentence.

At first, Rip meets a stranger. Then, he carries the barrel to help him. Later, he meets a number of men in old Dutch clothes. In the end, Rip goes to sleep.

When two things happen together, we can use at the same time.

3 Put the sentences in order. Then complete the sentences with the sequencing words from the box.

At first	At the same time	In the end	Later	Then

☐ **a** .... he sees a young man in his old coat – perhaps it is his son.

☐ **b** .... he tells the people of the town about the strange men in the mountains.

[1] **c** ..At first... Rip doesn't know the people in the town.

☐ **d** .... he goes to live with his daughter, and he tells his story to the visitors at the inn.

☐ **e** .... he talks to a young woman called Judith – his daughter!

4 Match these sentence halves correctly.

a	The horseman	**1**	is afraid of the headless horseman.
b	Brom	**2**	gallops away.
c	Gunpowder	**3**	throws his head at Ichabod.
d	People	**4**	marries Katrina.
e	Ichabod	**5**	find Ichabod's hat and a pumpkin near the bridge.

5 Write the sentences above in the story order using *At first, Then, At the same time, Later*, and *In the end*.

1 At first, Ichabod is afraid of the headless horseman.

2 ....

3 ....

4 ....

5 ....

GRAMMAR CHECK

Suffixes: –er and –ly

When we add the suffix –er to a verb (or –r when the verb ends in –e), we make a word for a person.

Katrina likes to sing and dance. She's a singer and a dancer.

When we add the suffix –ly to an adjective, we make an adverb about how we do something.

Ichabod is brave when he sings. He sings bravely.

When the adjective ends in consonant + –y, we change the y to i and add –ly.

Ichabod is hungry at the party. He eats hungrily.

When the adjective ends in consonant + short vowel + single consonant, we double the final consonant.

The students are careful when they work. They work carefully.

6 Add –r, –er, or –ly to the word in brackets to complete each sentence.

a It's easy for Ichabod to talk to the young women. He talks to them . .*easily*. . (easy)

b Ichabod teaches children. He's a .... (teach)

c Baltus likes to smoke. He's a .... (smoke)

d Brom's angry when he sees Katrina with Ichabod. He watches them .... (angry)

e Brom likes to fight. He's a .... (fight)

f It's wonderful to see Ichabod dance. He dances .... (wonderful)

g Ichabod tells the boys to go early. They leave school .... (happy)

h Brom rides a big strong horse. He's a good .... (ride)

i Ichabod's afraid. He speaks to the horseman .... (weak)

j Gunpowder's tired. He walks through the trees .... (slow)

k Now Gunpowder's galloping. He takes Ichabod across the bridge .... (quick)

GRAMMAR CHECK

Modal auxiliary verbs: can and can't

We use can + infinitive without *to* to talk about things we are able to do, and can't + infinitive without *to* to describe things that we are not able to do.

Katrina can sing.   *Brom can't dance.*

We don't use *do* in questions with can.

Can you ride a horse? ✓   *Do you can ride a horse?* ✗

Match the questions with the answers. Put the numbers in the boxes.

a Who can ride Daredevil? ☐7☐

b Who can Ichabod talk to easily? ☐

c How can Ichabod help the mothers of young children? ☐

d Why can't Ichabod see his book? ☐

e Who can sing and dance very well? ☐

f Why does the headless horseman always stop at the bridge? ☐

g Why can't Ichabod speak to the headless horseman? ☐

h What can people see near the bridge the next day? ☐

1 Because he's very afraid.

2 Ichabod can.

3 He can tell them stories.

4 Young women.

5 A hat and some pieces of pumpkin.

6 Because it's night time.

7 Brom can.

8 Because his horse can't step onto it.

GRAMMAR CHECK

Possessive 's and s'

We use 's and s' to talk about who things belong to.

With singular nouns, we use 's.   *rider – the rider's head*

With plural nouns, we use s'.   *farmers – the farmers' sons*

With irregular plural nouns, we use 's.   *women – the old women's stories*

8 Complete the sentences with the correct form of the word in brackets.

a The (children) children's teacher is Ichabod Crane.

b The (schoolboys) .... older sisters are beautiful.

c The (Van Tassels) .... farm is the biggest in the valley.

d Ichabod is (Katrina) .... singing teacher.

e (Brom) .... dog howls when Katrina sings.

f The (teacher) .... best suit is black.

g The (people) .... stories about ghosts are exciting.

h (Ichabod) .... hat is near the bridge.

i (Everyone) .... favourite story is the legend of Ichabod Crane and the Headless Horseman.

GRAMMAR CHECK

There is and there are

We use there is (there's) and there are to talk about the things and people in a place. We use there is with a singular noun, and there are with a plural noun.

There's a dog outside the school.

There are good things to eat on the table.

Complete the text with *there's* or *there are*.

In the picture a) there's a valley, and b) .... some hills. On the left
c) .... a road. d) ...., some houses in the picture, and e) .... some
little farm buildings too. At the front of the picture f) .... two women, and near
the women g) .... a white dog. h) .... a white cat next to the dog.
i) .... lots of trees in the picture. On some of the trees j) .... white
flowers, and on some of the trees k) .... red apples. In front of one house
l) .... a white horse. On the left of the picture m) .... a man. He's
working in his garden.

⫽DOMINOES THE STRUCTURED APPROACH TO READING IN ENGLISH⫽

Dominoes is an enjoyable series of illustrated classic and modern stories in four carefully graded language stages – from Starter to Three – which take learners from beginner to intermediate level.

Each *Domino* reader includes:
- a **good story** to read and enjoy
- **integrated activities** to develop reading skills and increase active vocabulary
- **personalized projects** to make the language and story themes more meaningful
- **seven pages of grammar activities** for consolidation.

Each *Domino* pack contains a reader, plus a MultiROM with:
- a **complete audio recording of the story**, fully dramatized to bring it to life
- **interactive activities** to offer further practice in reading and language skills and to consolidate learning.

If you liked this Starter Level *Domino*, why not read these?

Tristan and Isolde
Retold by Bill Bowler

Tristan and Isolde are in love, but Isolde must marry King Mark. So a happy love story seems impossible . . .

The lovers meet every day but then, one night, King Mark finds them together. Now Tristan must leave the castle, but he is badly hurt and dying. Only Isolde can help him.

Can Isolde find Tristan in time? Can their love survive?

Book ISBN: 978 0 19 424713 9
MultiROM Pack ISBN: 978 0 19 424677 4

A Pretty Face
John Escott

Zoe Baker works in a bookstore. She also likes acting, and she has a part in the play *Romeo and Juliet*. Mike Morrison writes about the play for the newspaper. What does he write about Zoe? Is Zoe a good actress . . . or is she just 'a pretty face'?

What does Zoe think when she reads the newspaper? What does she do?

Book ISBN: 978 0 19 424704 7
MultiROM Pack ISBN: 978 0 19 424668 2

You can find details and a full list of books in the *Dominoes* catalogue and Oxford English Language Teaching Catalogue, and on the website: www.oup.com/elt

Teachers: see www.oup.com/elt for a full range of online support, or consult your local office.

	CEF	Cambridge Exams	IELTS	TOEFL iBT	TOEIC
Starter	A1	YLE Movers	–	–	–
Level 1	A1–A2	YLE Flyers/KET	3.0	–	–
Level 2	A2–B1	KET-PET	3.0-4.0	–	–
Level 3	B1	PET	4.0	57-86	550